papîyâhtak

papîyâhtak

RITA BOUVIER

thistledown press

National Library of Canada Cataloguing in Publication

Bouvier, Rita E.
Papîyâhtak / Rita Bouvier.

Poems.
ISBN 1-894345-69-X

1. Cree Indians--Poetry. 2. Métis--Poetry. I. Title.

PS8553.O8893P36 2004   C811'.54   C2004-900862-5

Cover embroidery sample stitched by Flora (Gardiner)Bouvier.
Photo credit: Gabriel Dumont Institute
Cover and book design by J. Forrie
Typeset by Thistledown Press

Thistledown Press Ltd.
633 Main Street
Saskatoon, Saskatchewan, S7H 0J8
www.thistledown.sk.ca

Thistledown Press gratefully acknowledges the financial assistance of the Canada Council for the Arts, the Saskatchewan Arts Board, and the Government of Canada through the Book Publishing Industry Development Program for its publishing program.

for the children

CONTENTS

papîyâhtak

bannock and oranges

winter is certain

papîyâhtak

to act in a thoughtful way,
a respectful way,
a joyful way,
a balanced way

Gabriel Dumont Overture

the first movement

thunder rolls a darkened sky
it'll be rain for sure
as wind gathers strength
I am rounding the bend
when along comes Gabriel
riding frozen along the bank

he beckons âstam ôta   come over here
tears like raindrops welling
as I move closer and closer

the hand that cast the statue
in memory of him
could not have had a heart
why is he laden in steel?
I caress his aching back
afraid he might turn

he is travelling westward
his sight set on the far beyond
and when we part I swear
his eyes alight as they meet mine
the horse he rides neighing
as the sky opens

the portrait

I say I am

my grandfather is flashing brilliance
against a dark sky.

my grandmother is the calm
forgiving after the storm.

my aunt is a birch basket
she catches all.

my grandfather says
I am an angel
sent by St Peter
to guide him
when he loses his way.

my grandmother says
I am 'î kîmôtât sit' —
the one who lives under
hiding secrets.

my aunt says
I am a daughter
a daughter for all.

I say, I am. I say
I am all these things
and much, much more.

the portrait

the portrait she holds for others to see
is a likeness of mama and papa
"Dick, Jane — that's me, and Sally
our pets, Puff and Spot, to be sure."
but she is unrecognizable
in this perfect life
idyllic summers on Waskesieu Lake
winters away, somewhere in the Bahamas
but she tells this story anyway
it's the right one, to be sure.

underneath this
cracked and peeling
as if someone had folded it
in half and then again
for safe-keeping, perhaps
is a glimpse of a young girl
her teeth whitened
from the hardened resin
of the spruce tree
smiling at an old man
a pipe in hand, standing
in a bed of wild roses
bluebells and fireweed.

behind them trails wind
into the tall brush in all directions
opening one door to the other. Eden.
all finding their way
to the lake that surrounds them.

and there, outside the frame
she is to him as he is to her
an oarsman to a fisherman
   apprentice to a soap-maker
   assistant to a canoe-builder
a magician at shaping forms
to stretch each pelt of fur
he has caught and sent her way.

but here in the foreground
too close for the camera's eye
a poet sits alone
far, far away from home
in dark, Gucci sunglasses
a pure touch of silk on cotton
she has become accustomed to

weeping in Starbucks
on Denman Street.

I am created
(for my father, Emile)

I am created by a natural bond
between a man and a woman,
but this one, is forever two.
one is white, the Other, red.
a polarity of being, absorbed
as one. I am nature with clarity.

against my body, white rejects red
and red rejects white. instinctively,
I have learned to love — I have learned to live
though the politics of polarity
is never far away. still, I am
waiting, waiting.

Pointe la Roche

she remembers the day like it was
yesterday — dark, the wind howling
whitecaps on the lake. the day she ran away
to Pointe La Roche — a fury ignited from
the sting of words — she was — *konita awâsis.*   a child in vain
a church proclamation — she learned later
one conversation in her mother's bed
too late, too late the damage done.

she remembers the very day like it was
carved into her skull — her body burning
carrying her over the footsteps of stones
the edge where the land meets the water.
as the waves broke around her feet, grandfather
appeared, sat beside her — took his hat off,
his wrinkled hands coming to rest on his lap
a sign he would be staying for a while.

a thirst unquenched

the next time she heard from him was by foot,
he was drunk. his messenger said he was
asking, asking for her to come quickly
he wanted her to come — to come and pick
up the pieces, so he could start over, again.

she remembers she was just ten, then.
he was a haunting sight, eyes half closed
a twisted face, parched lips and a dry tongue.
the signs of consumption; a thirst unquenched.

when she came to his rescue, as he knew
she would, she remembers the sparkle in his eye.
she an angel in disguise. she lifted him.
together they struggled to stay on the narrow path
to face grandmother's wrath and holy ghosts.

a spider tale

behind the shed
in the tall yellow grass
a cardboard box
is my make-believe home
no one can see me
but I can see
                        all
their comings
            and goings

my auntie Albertine
is washing clothes today
and needs the power
of my long arms
and lanky legs
to haul pails and pails
of water from the lake

I watch
            as she searches for me
mumbles something about
kihtimigan — that lazy one
walks back inside the house
            and out again
calling my name

when I appear
out of nowhere
she looks relieved to see me

"nitânis, tânitê oma î ḵîtotîyin?"   my daughter, where in the world have you been?
I tell her —
I was here all along

what I don't tell her is
that I have been spinning tales
trying to understand
the possibility of . . .
myself as a spider
        all legs
travelling here and there
with disturbing speed
my preoccupation food
my home a web
so intricate and fragile
yet strong as sinew

today I remembered
not as sure footed
as I would like to be
someone calling my name
I lost my footing
falling, falling

sailing the deep

I will take with me
miyomaskihkî — sacred medicine

    nimoshôm'pan — my late grandfather
    a way of being with you in silence

    nimâmâ — my mother
    a presence at the end of the line

    ninâpîm — my one man
    a good love like no other

    noḵosis — my son
    a tale of spiders in rubber suction boots

    nisîmis — my younger sibling
    a belief there is always room for one more

    niwîcîwâḵanak — the ones with whom I make a path
    a reading of the great mystery

    nohkom'pan — my late grandmother
    a prayer when there is no where else to turn

dark like me

a Cree soliloquy

what kind of a human being is this
that hates so much; what kind of a human
being is this, that wants to destroy its —
self and the gifts offered? does it not have

enough — to eat, does it not have shelter
over its head — to keep it warm at night,
does it not have love — to nurture it, does
it not understand its relations?

what is it afraid of? to starve — to suffer
from the freezing cold — to live without
the love of another human being —
to die, perhaps to die — to die alone

yet, it destroys the essence of itself
winged, finned, crawler, four legged
the water, the air that keeps it alive
the greening of life, of desire — to live

here, now

I have been standing here on the hillside
heart-pounding having just witnessed thousands
upon thousands of buffalo slain, left
there writhing, squealing on the ground to die

unable to comprehend men surveying
my land, then erecting fences and signs
I have been standing here on the roadside
reading, *no trespassing — private property*

on road allowance, waiting for a ride
wanting in, growing weary and numb
from a long bitter cold, standing there
you offer, *I hear anger in your voice*

disconnected landscaped lines

a stranger is standing in the middle
of a sidewalk in distress. it could be
any city but it is not. it is the city
of the homeless, San Francisco.

every galley, alley, a remnant
of a lost soul's bed. every galley,
alley, a reminder it could be me.
it could be me, I remind myself!

on the street, hand over mouth
a woman is repeating over and over
to any passer-by who will listen
"what can I do? oh dear!

what can I do? oh dear!
I simply can't leave him there to die.
I simply can't leave him there to die?
what can I do? oh dear!"

I stop, curious, cityscape distrusting —
potted lit trees and hollow rhythms
of steel, glass and concrete. I stop.
"he's hurt" she says as our eyes meet.

"what can we do? oh dear!
what can we do? oh dear!"
when I notice the winged creature,
an urban dweller, with mangled legs

and wings, rolling over and over
on the concrete bed. I reach out —
holding her grief in my arms.
I promise to stay until help comes.

dark like me

at the corner of College and Mckinnon
I stop for a red light.
a habit of mind, thank God!
the traffic tonight a steady solid stream.

and then, out of nowhere a man appears.
in an accented voice, he claims he is lost.
he is seeking a place, last night's aromas
of coffees and teas from around the world.

I direct him to Broadway Avenue.
we make small talk from Afghanistan
via Bulgaria to Canada. he is here to study
crop science genetics and would like to stay.

and then, the conversation shifts
you are dark like me, he observes.
I am Metis I declare, and offer
additional explanation. he declines.

he says he has been to Batoche
to the gravesite, to the little church
and he knows the story. as if
Batoche held the only story.

but when we part his words are a song,
you are dark like me, you are dark like me
I say over and over again, in time
to the rhythm of my breathing

my arms and legs in full motion, I run
the bridges tonight, like never before.
later that evening, in search of friends
the deck at Earls, when the hostess inquires,
"is one of them blond?"
I reply without hesitation
"no, they are dark like me.
they are dark like me."

a science dialogue

a stranger asked me
will you be okay?

and memory unravelled
time into place — *wânaskêwin*   a place to be at peace with oneself

I remember a distant voice
asking aloud, *"is there order?"*
I was thinking it was
a question, out of time

I was thinking then, the universe
just is — alive
takes my breath away

the voice insisting
"who cares? do we really know?
what does it mean to know?"

I was thinking, I know
we belong to a great mystery
the moon, you and I are one.

"think," said the voice
"where are you, when you think?
the Navajo say, where I stand
is where I think.
thought is expansive
as the universe."

my heart quickened, I was thinking
of what happens when thought
is void of place, when time

is void of place, when time
is without rhythm —
earth, sun, sky and moon
and my heart is breaking

that voice again:
"how do you reconcile
the measure of time with stars
older than the universe?"
too many questions
coming too, too fast

I was thinking time is a cycle
and I am hoping
child-like for tomorrow

and that stranger asked
will you be okay?

it was then, I told him this story
how time had extended —
a suspended moon
wept, washing over me

it was then, I told him this story
how the sun rose
early this morning
winked, and only I could see

Indigenous man

piercing hazel eyes, he walks into the room
commanding attention, claiming devastation
of cultural capital, when educated, indigenous
women marry outside the community.

as one woman seated in the circle today
I raise my voice in protest, women
not the only ones guilty of this crime
if it is one — a phenomena including indigenous men.

reconciled, I write to remember —

I see in your gait the walk of a proud man.
I hear in your voice, a gentle call to your side.
and when our eyes meet, I understand the joy
and the pain we share on opposite sides of the world.

your eyes are a mirror that tell me I am beautiful
as I have never ever imagined before. yet,
there is a hint of a struggle not yet over.
and I am waiting for that moment when

our touching eyes meet again,
when I see love for yourself.
I will know then that you are the one,
the one I have been dreaming!

nipîkiskwân

I speak, not of cows with halos
but of matters unspoken, corruption
reactionary politics
exclusivity and primacy
of one group over another
the language of *'race'*

I speak, of oppressive forces
we replicate in our actions
to silence difference —
suppressive rule
among the poorest
of a people on the land

I speak, of romantic myths
we perpetuate in our struggle
to be human, to be human
beads and feathers
holier than thou
looks and attitudes

I speak, of nationalistic hymns
we sing in our desire
for harmonious living
First Nation — Metis Nation
a false sense of being
one, with each other
in our mother's home

we say we want it all

we fight amongst ourselves
jealous, one of us is standing.

there are no celebrations
for brave deeds among the chaos, instead

we join the banner call for rights
forgetting an idea from the past —

responsibility. we join the march
for freedom, forgetting an idea

from the past — peace keeping.
we say we want, want it all

a piece of the action we know destroys
our home — our relations with each other

we are mired so deep, drowning
in our own thinking, thinking

we too could have it all, if only . . .
if only we could see ourselves

Riel is dead, and I am alive

I listen passively while strangers
claim monopoly of the truth.
one claims *Riel is hero,*
while the other insists, *Riel was mad.*

I can feel a tension rising, a sterile talk
presenting the life of a living people,
sometime in eighteen eighty five.
now, some time in nineteen ninety five

a celebration of some odd sort.
I want to scream. listen you idiots,
Riel is dead! and I am alive!
instead, I sit there mute and voiceless.

the truth unravelling, as academics
parade their lines, and cultural imperialists
wave their flags. this time the gatling gun
is academic discourse, followed

by a weak response of political rhetoric.
all mumbo-jumbo for a past, that is
irreconcilable. this much I know
when I remember — I remember

my mother — her hands tender, to touch
my grandmother — her eyes, blue, the sky
my great grandmother — a story, a star gazer
who could read plants, animals and the sky.

a Metis soldier remembers Dumont

a few of us had decided to retreat
into the large wood with Riel
to continue the fight,
or what was left of it,
against *les Canadiens*.
as we were leaving Riel said to Dumont
"we are beaten, my friend."

I remember — Dumont's words to Riel
as if he had chosen them, carefully.

nîcwâm, kâwiya nântaw itihta   my brother — my friend, don't be disheartened
when we picked up our guns
we knew we would not win this fight.
when peaceful interventions
to protect our land are ignored
and there is no place
north, east, south or west
to make our home
what else could we have done?
at least, we can say
we held our heads high."

as we were leaving Riel then said to Dumont,
"be careful, be careful my friend."
to which Dumont replied,
"*tâpwî!*, but they can't kill me, Riel.   it might be so

but pray for me, just in case."

remembering old man Oulette

in the Battle of Batoche we held our own
as best as we could without ammunition.
we had dug trenches along the ridge
of the river bank and from that location
we were able to restrain our enemy
for some time.

as ammunition ran low we used nails
against our enemy; the gatling gun
on their side. *les fou!* that we were!
I can tell you now we were no match
for the Canadian militia who had come —
were sent to make an example of us.

I will always remember the final day of battle
as we scrambled out of the trenches
to save our pitiful lives. there was an old man
old Joseph Oulette, ninety three years of age
who stayed behind in the trenches. according to him
"to kill one more Englishman".

mon dieux! have mercy on his soul!

that was a long time ago, and we are here today

that was a long time ago
and we are here today

listen, listen
the heart of the land beats

blood was spilled
and it stained the earth
leaving a mark

history as it is written
attempts to speak one truth
as if facts spoke for themselves

listen, listen
the heart of the land beats

our children curious
as all children are
will ask the the right questions

why does a nation take up arms
in a battle knowing it will lose?
knowing it will lose

listen, listen
the heart of the land beats

when the long night turns to day
remember, hope is the morning
a songbird's prayer

to dance is dangerous

the humid scent of earth fills my nostrils
my feet pounding on soft grass, soft rhythms
transporting me into a spirit world.

grandmothers, grandfathers, talking incongruence
of words and actions. they tell me, return
return to the language that conveys the meaning.
power is not control over; power is
volition — a sacred act of intention.

they tell me return, return to the teachings
of the ancient ones — the sun, the moon, the stars
the earth — its rivers, its stones, its medicines.
dance to remember; the most dangerous one
lurks inside each of us, diminishing
capacity to forge a vision many can embrace.

my re-entry is painful I want to stay
to stay in a spirit world, forever.

Gabriel Dumont Overture

the second movement

the sun has disappeared, dusk
brings a calm to the day
darkness waits on the edge
my sadness laden in steel
my mind tormented
last night's dream, vivid.

I am fixed-time identity
searching, where passion might
meet compassion down the line.

in dream — one moment
I am holding the key, but
I can't find the right door
among many. the next moment
I see a steel door before me
but not one of the keys I hold, fit.

tonight, I hope and pray
Gabriel won't notice me
passing in the dark.
then I turn, catching him
high above the saddle
waving, holding tight rein
the wind caught in his hair.

would I do it again?

I sold it for twenty dollars
at a pawn shop
on twentieth and avenue D.
it wasn't worth that much,
I would have given it away.

when I arrived he was busy
counting the bills at the till.
how much?, he says, monotone
twenty dollars sir, is all I want.
nothing more. nothing more.
twenty dollars?, are you sure?
he asks, unable to hide his surprise
twenty dollars sir, I reply.

I sold it, my heart encased in stone.
would I do it again?
perhaps keep the diamond
and have it reset,
or maybe sell for a higher price?

no. I'd sell it again
for the exact same price
at the same pawn shop, if I could.
only this time, I'd sell it
for the woman I have become.

all the while, I was losing ground

while I ran to the rhythmic beat of
a distant place far, far away. the sun
rose to its greatest height and argued
with the wind chill about who was mightier
and all the while, I was losing ground
the snow and ice melting beneath my feet.

that's three for you

a young man came to me one day wanting
to understand me — the distance between
separate worlds, his and mine, his and mine.
surely, he begged, we could forsake the past
for the future, yours and mine, yours and mine.

I listened intently trying to find
the right words to say, to reassure him
my intentions, telling my story — the same.
I told him perhaps the past remembered
holds our future, yours and mine, yours and mine.

I wish it was as easy to forget
as it is, writing this poem for you.
I wish I could believe, I wish we could
break this damn cycle of separate worlds.
I wish I wish I wish. that's three for you.

even Metis women get the blues

I am a grey sky
with no sun in sight.
I am an abandoned home
on the roadside
northbound
on this Saturday
spring-like morning
on my way to work;
my mother on my mind
wishing my sister here.
I sway to the music
a tune about somebody
saying they were sorry.

I am wings spread
flying, soaring empty
î kitimâkihtamân   in a state of impoverishment
nothing like Cree
to express my state of mind.
I am coming down
a night of friendship
connecting the lines
of our sacred lives
a night of laughter
lost loves — lost lives;
foolish crazy thoughts
of women with children.

I sway to the music
a lonely tune about
nothing being sadder
than losing yourself
in love.

like I've said before
even Metis women
get the blues, sometimes.

out on starry night

oh lucky me I say pinching myself.
John Kim Bell is standing before me
extending a hand, while I stammer
trying to find the right words.
pleased to be here I say.
he smiles, shakes my hand.
the Saskatchewan Hotel tonight
transformed into Indian Country.

lounging at a table or so, away
is Tantoo Cardinal and all her friends.
me? well, I am sitting alone.
this is nothing unusual.

the next time, I dare my eyes to look,
I spot Gordon beside Tantoo.
you know, Gordon Tootoosis
constellation, Big Bear.
star shining bright in the distant sky.

wanting more, I search the night
hoping to catch a rising star.
I notice him. he could make
an old woman's eyes hurt so bad.
Michael Greyeyes, nonchalant
pony tailed, starched white shirt
blue jeans and all, sitting at a table
with all his friends, no less.

as the stars fade into the dark spaces
I'm still sitting alone, but feeling okay
just admiring as I've done

many times before on my back porch.
I'm thinking, the next thing you know
Maria Campbell, she will show.
Maria, she's a friend, a wishing star.

leaving the lounge, a couple glasses
of wine away, I am uncertain
of what I'd say if I bumped into
a constellation, so to speak.
what does one say?
tansi! I've seen you in the movies.   hello, how are you!
tansi! I've read your books.
tansi! I know your medicine.

wouldn't you know, standing in the shadows
with all his friends and followers
is Howard Adams, star strident.
I say, Howard, it's me, its me!
remember me? I came to see you
seeking wisdom. he remembers.
I believe him. tonight I will believe anything.

the next evening in a celebration,
the achievements of our honoured guests
we make entry, a Grand Entry
into the spotlight. I'm flying high
brushing tips with so many stars
and would be stars.

as night descends I hear the buzz
of a shoooooting star. it's Murray Porter
of *1492, Who Found Who* — Columbus blue.
wah ! wah! what a night it's going to be!

last night at Lydia's

Celtic toe-tapping fiddle
Red River jigging rhythm
runs in my veins
a surge like lightning

that testosterone
in the mix tonight.
ohhhh, it feels good
to be alive

plaid shirted, tight blue jeans
good-looking, knows it kind-a-man
you hurt my eyes

pony-tailed, dark skinned
women in arm kind-a-man
you hurt my eyes

rugged, canoe-paddling
handsome kind-a-man
you hurt my eyes

muscle busting, v-necked
silver buckled kind-a-man
you hurt my eyes

cool, leathered, scotch-sipping
drinking kind-a-man
you hurt my eyes

quiet, wire-rimmed
spectacled kind-a-man
you hurt my eyes

you — you — you —
holding my hand kind-a-man
ohhhh, you hurt my eyes

papîyâhtak

Ernestine remembers

when the battle was over
we remained in hiding
along the river valley
the river, our life blood.
                    unsure,
what would become of us.
                    unsure,
what was in store,
now and in the future.

les Canadiens   military force under General Middleton
had destroyed
what little we owned,
stolen precious items
from our humble homes
never to be returned.
some may say that
all is fair in war
then, perhaps its true.

we knew Gabriel and Riel
if they were alive
would be taken as prisoners.
there would be
no one to speak for us
against a power
that seemed relentless.

â nikiskisin, nîsta　　　　　　　　　but I remember, too
on that first night
after the battle of Batoche
no sooner had we
made a bed of straw
to settle for the long night
the younger ones
crying from hunger
when Dumont appeared
out of nowhere
as he had done
throughout the battle.

he held out for all to see
little moccasins
which he had sewn.
his hands raised
over his head
as if it were an offering
to kisî-man'tô　　　　　　　　　the kind, loving creator

he claimed, thus, making it so
that while the Canadians
were taking practice shots
cîpayak î nîmihitotwâw　　　　　　the ghosts dancing
"I sewed these little moccasins
for the children
to keep them warm, tonight
to keep them warm tonight"

mama, did God create me?

(in memory of Marcile Gratton, ten years old —
a casuality of the Battle of Batoche.)

mama, did God create me?

> *nitanis,* God created you and loves you   my daugther
> everything in creation is good.

mama, why are we hiding?
I want to go home
I'm scared, *mama,* I'm scared.

> I'm scared too, my girl
> but everything will be all right
> you stay under the blanket
> it's getting very cold
> and it will be a long night.
> I am going to look for firewood.

> you look at the stars
> and I'll be back
> before you know it.

mama, I can touch the stars.

our children

I heard a voice calling
late one night,
it was a woman's voice.
our children are dying
our children are dying
the voice cried,
from wasted excesses
p o l l u t i o n.
this morning I read
the Beluga whale
lies in the Gulf
of the St Lawrence
dying, poisoned.

I heard a voice calling
again late last night,
this time it was a man.
our children are dying
our children are dying
the voice cried,
from wasted excesses
g l o b a l i z a t i o n.
this morning I read
Dolly is suffering
from a disease of old age —
a genetic clitch?

tonight I'm calling
our children are dying
our children are dying.

papîyâhtak
(dedicated to the children)

if you ever have the chance
to lick salt with cows, join them
otherwise, you will never make a friend.

go swimming in a puddle
with all your clothes on;
for no reason, other than
that it feels good.

use your little pinky
melt a hole on the frosted window
to see the pinpoint of your father
returning home from work;
run to him and when
he scoops you into the air
fly, just for that moment
he won't let go — I promise you.

hide from the adults all day
pretend you don't hear them;
when they ask where you were
say, *nowhere.*

lie on the rooftop with your mother
watching the moon and the stars
wondering how far away, is far;
it's zany

go dancing in the park
after a rain with all your friends
with only your pajamas on;

it's entertaining for the people
caught inside their houses

save all the earthworms you find
on the sidewalk after a rain;
return each and every one
to the place they know best;
you never know
when you might need a helping hand.

bury all the dead birds in your path
find a special place for each of them
preferably in the garden;
you just never know

it's okay, steal peanut butter
and bread from the pantry
while the nuns are sleeping;
there are worse crimes one can commit.

when your mother tells you
that she loves you to the moon
and back times infinity
try to out-do the immensity
of the love she describes to you;
there really is no end to it.

finally, believe what you say
or don't say anything at all;
it is better that way.

dear tap tap, c/o St Peter

I have been counting my fortunes
hoping for grandchildren someday
far away, from the time when *Weetigo*   The Hungry One
frightened the children away
far away, from the swirling water
that might have swallowed them up.

> *Moshôm, that was really you*
> *in the fish box, wasn't it?*
> *it really wasn't* Weetigo, *was it?*

Weetigo moved to the city, you know
when Matthew Joseph learned to walk.
afraid he might lose his way in the alleys,
Weetigo was always around the corner.
afraid he might follow Donatello
down the sewers into the Saskatchewan,
Weetigo made his home in the sewer
far away from adults but close to children.

> *Moshôm, that was really you*
> *in the fish box, wasn't it?*
> *it really wasn't* Weetigo, *was it?*

in the bathtub late one night, unafraid
he was prepared to hear the story
of *Weetigo* — The Hungry One.
and so the story unravelled
of the human being who chose to live

a selfish life, a life without care.
banished, he roams, a changed hideous form
aimlessly looking for children to eat.

> *Moshôm, that was really you*
> *in the fish box, wasn't it?*
> *it really wasn't* Weetigo, *was it?*

hand on hand

we made a pact but you were only three.
I was so much older I should have known
better. I promised then to take care of you
as long as my hands were bigger than yours.

in return, you promised to take care of —
me, when your hands would grow bigger than mine.
today, you came to me wanting to measure
your hand against mine; I said, go away

your hands growing way, way too fast for me.
just then, a thick fog descended across
the street. you ran into it curious
unafraid, unaware you were disappearing

with every step you took. I ran after you
trying as best as I could to hold on
with you in sight, letting go at each step.
hand on hand we made a pact, you were three.

space is an emptiness

I awaken, sensing a need to fill
the space with song — my mother's peppermint tea
books that inspire the soul, books with heart.
space is an emptiness of going through
the motions of giving, not receiving
of longing for family and friendship.

on my favourite chair the vividness
of colour slowly returns as the light
shifts. the soft shuffle of feet announcing
your presence, your voice is this morning's song.
mama, you call, *mama are you there?*

I know this, if you had not awakened
I would have unconsciously raised the volume
of the music, to hasten your coming —
to find that comfortable spot upon
my lap, so we could read and talk of
sunday morning dreams and nightly monsters.

young fisherman in Mexico

the young ones are caught
in a web, like fish to bait
as fishermen cast their net along the shore
and pelicans dive on easy prey

the young man, city born and bred
lying beside me on the beach, a moment ago
is a fisherman now
as he pulls a net to shore

without one word of exchange
he knows the part he must play
he pulls hand over hand
mimicking motions
he, the pelicans and the fisherman
of Ricon de Guayabitos
performing a tribal custom

the performance over
he feeds the pelicans discarded fish
hand to mouth, a friendship cast
by the fishermen and their net

next, he is running toward me
breathless, delighted in his discovery
he claims, landing beside me
mama, we should stay — Here, forever

my dear Emerson

my dear Emerson, I wrote these lines
the morning after our journey together
so I could remember — maybe
remind you someday of that time
you and I took a trip together
through the city, beyond the prairies
and into the trees one late autumn day.

mama, had called to say, she was
missing you, could I bring you along
on the trip home. at first, I must admit
I was a little reluctant, maybe afraid.

when I swung by to pick you up
you were waiting, waiting for me
all two and a half feet high
of bright eyes, no luggage
smart talk and a soulful sway.

as I remember you came willingly
leaving your mother arms into mine
still, I was unsure if a five hundred kilometer trip
with a two year old was a good idea.

as we turned the corner onto the busy street
you announced that *papa* Louis
had driven by in his truck,
smiled and then waved at you.
I wasn't sure of what to say to you.

I took the risk and said that *papa* Louis
had left this earth — a euphemism for dead

hoping you understood. your eyes a quiver
you scolded me, affirming it was *papa* Louis
the licence plate on his truck had said so
and then we spoke about *papa* Louis
how we missed him, vowing to keep him
in our hearts forever.

time flew away. where? I don't know for sure.
we painted portraits of the people
we loved, *mama* and *papa* Louis.
we painted pictures of things we loved
rainbows and butterflies, flowers and bugs.
we painted our favourite foods
bananas and strawberries, oranges and apples
and then we sang songs — happy songs, sad songs
until you fell into a deep sleep.

when you awoke we started all over again
singing and laughing, laughing and singing
like two silly drunks off a trapline.
lost to the world, I said, Emerson
come home with me — come and stay with me.
then you gave me the saddest of eyes
said you would miss *mama*.

I am sorry my words frightened you
made you sad. I tried to explain
I didn't really mean it that way
I just wanted to tell you how much

I loved you, how much joy you were
on this autumn afternoon, where
real and dream are entangled as one.

for a moment I forgot you were only two
three soon, you told me waving three
chubby little fingers in my face so I could see.

wanting to make it up to you I said, listen
listen to my voice — E m e r s o n
I said your name aloud ever so slowly
again, E m e r s o n.

it is a beautiful name I said more directly
and you laughed at me, told me I was funny
very, very funny. your laughter filling
the van, spilling over all over the world.

you, my dear Emerson are my teacher
thank you for the joy in my heart that day
it is forever etched on this piece of paper
I sign it with my name, *auntie*
auntie with hearts in her eyes.

the postscript reads:
we kiss goodnight
with moose meat on your lips.

Gabriel Dumont Overture

the final movement

the sun sets the sky on fire
the wind without sail
tomorrow will be a great day
slowly I climb
the steep height of the bridge
my head in the clouds

tonight I am conscious
of decay around me
my own complicity

compelled, I turn again
to the frozen rider
on the river bank, and
Gabriel's eyes meet mine
once again, reminding me
I am not alone

I smile, wave him onward.
he tips his hat
gives a slight downward nod.
we part eyes on fire,
the horse he rides neighing
as darkness falls a new day

Ghiraradelli Square
(San Francisco, California, 1999)

my eyes closed
blood red
in the mid day sun.
the Andes flute
floats melodious notes
high on the mountaintop
such depth of sound
in a breath of longing.
thunder cracks the drum
lightning, then rain awash
on playful hollow steel.

I soar home
from the mountaintop
to my beloved
a les Bouleau
a perfumed garden
of wild roses, bluebells
and wild fireweed
my cousins and I
chasing rabbits and squirrels
to their hiding places.

the rustling whisper
of dry seeded pods
brings me back, clouds rolling
birds chirping
picking the seeds
on the earth
beneath my feet.

revelation

there was revelation, a sudden beauty
on my run this morning. a frigid icy
temperature clinging to the bright sun,
shining held fast, warm against my face.

flowing below me an open, steady
defiant stream of raging river power
against the odds of a wintry depth.
a winter so cold, my ears were tinkling.

all of a sudden I had a surge of
strength — an unyielding rage of power
I was running, a celebratory
run, reassured of a greater power

bannock and oranges

the alarm clock sounds
far, far away, uncertain
of place, perhaps too many
hotel rooms. I can't count.

they are all the same
a dull bedspread here
a bedside table there.
lamps, always too many
a chair for company
that never arrives.
an empty, dank smell
everywhere I turn; me
wishing I was home
except this morning.

something on the table
catches the morning light
memory brings clarity.
bannock and oranges
still, against a backdrop
of freshly washed linen
as I had left them late
last night when I returned
to my nowhere hotel room
after a visit with my mom.

a schooled eye can see
that what was once ordinary

is not so in morning light
the preparation like communion
between your wrinkled hands.

I remember watching you
slice the bannock — aroma fresh
toasting it medium, and then
buttering it, sparingly
my unique preference
among nine siblings
juice spurting on your hands
as you sectioned oranges
placed them in a scrubbed
plastic recycled yogurt tub
so I would not go without

no still life can be more beautiful than
bannock wrapped in freshly washed
pressed white linen graced with
sectioned oranges in a recycled yogurt tub

cab driver

you greet me and treat me with such kindness
offering me a tour of Halifax
the place you have come to call your home

on the ride through the city streets
you point out the right places to see
 and the places I should avoid alone

and then you tell me a story, of blacks
you despise them, a bunch of lazy thieves
how can I share who I really am

beneath this veneer of cloth, finely woven
beneath this veneer of skin, lightly touched
I am more sad than angry, sad than angry

you can not see
the colour of soul

when the silence breaks

I am a reluctant speaker
violence not just a physical thing.

words are one thing
I can hold them in my hand
later embroider them
like you do fine silk
on white deer hide
if I want.
but dead silence
that's another matter
there is nothing to hold on to
like the falling
before you awaken.

I imagine it this way, simply
kitahtawî êkwa   one of these days now
when the silence breaks
the deer will stop in their tracks
pausing eyes wide
the wolverine will roll over and over
on the hillside, and
you will hear my voice
as if for the first time
distant and then melodic
and you will recognize it
as your very own.

kitahtawî êkwa

letter to a friend

(in dedication to my late grandmother, Flora, whose faith in the goodness of humanity was unwavering, especially for those who dedicated their lives to Kisî man'tô — the kind, loving creator of all — Father Lacombe, Bishop Tache, Father Rossignol, Sister Beaudoin, Father Moreau etc.)

my dear friend,
as the railway trails its way
                              west
there is unrest among the Indians
                    and the Metis.

Louis Riel has appeared
on the Canadian scene
                    once again
                    a thorn
in the side of government.

the government has nearly
completed its operation
of impounding the Cree,

but Big Bear is no one's fool.

the Indians are in a sad state
throughout *the Northwest.*   historic Canadian place name of a vast region
living in confined spaces.   including what is now Saskatchewan.
many are starving
rations, having been withheld.

a blind government
has sent small foolish men
to lord over them.

all the while settlers arrive
on promised land

splashing upon its valleys
and washing over it ridges.

what will become of the Indian?

land on which the Metis live
has been surveyed
the Metis fear
their land will be taken
                sub-divided
against their wishes
                once again.
a people can not raise their young
                homeless.
a people can not live on air
                alone.

what will become of the Metis?

the Metis, who have treated us
                like family
now show distrust for us
questioning our loyalty.

the government is not
                without blame
                having ignored
all their petitions to be heard.

on this winter, star lit night
the beauty of *Kiwetin* shines.   district of the north wind
I pray for you and wish you well.

your friend, Father LaCombe
December 1884

62

I mean no disrespect

" . . . And whereas the said Indians have been notified and informed by Her
Majesty's said Commmissioners that it is the desire of Her Majesty to open
settlement, immigration and other such purposes as to Her Majesty may seem
meet, a tract of country, bounded and described as hereinafter mentioned, and to
obtain the consent hereto of her Indian subjects inhabiting the said tract, and to
make a treaty and arrange with them, so that there may be peace and goodwill
between them and Her Majesty, and that they may know and be assured of what
allowance they are to count upon and receive from Her Majesty's bounty and
benevolence; . . . "
(Excerpt from the Hon. Alexander Morris, P.C. Late Lieutenant-Governor
of Manitoba, The Northwest Territories and KEE-WA-TIN, Treaties of
Canada with the Indians, originally published in 1862.)

I hope you will understand, why
I refuse to take the ten steps it takes
from my favourite chair
to my die-for balcony view
to wave the queen on her visit
to the beautiful — *miyōsin*
Saskatoon, Saskatchewan

I mean no disrespect
she is probably a lovely lady
but I am too busy
trying to make sense
of a people and a democracy
that claims to uphold the rights
of all men, while women struggle
for recognition as persons

I am too busy
trying to understand
the meaning of treaty
a promise of peace —

miyo-wîcihitowin   a sacred act of good relations
so all children would learn
to live side by side, yet —

all I see around me
children in poverty
injustices defended
tax breaks for the rich
hidden taxes for the poor
a grovelling greed
based on a dollar bill
with her picture on it

the man said

the number one problem we face
is the growing population
of Aboriginal people, the man said
as he looked around scanning.
if we don't do something
to help these people, now
our children will carry the burden
of a future workforce that is
under-educated, under-
under-employed, the man said
hoping to get my vote

now don't get me wrong, he said
our party has many of these people
working with us, working with us
words chosen carefully, in case

the second issue is taxation, the man said
as you know, these people do not pay taxes
and if they were to pay taxes — contribute
their fair share to the provincial coffers
we would all benefit, them and us
words chosen carefully, in case

now don't get me wrong, he said
lower taxation, of course is the overall goal
for all taxpayers in this province
I want my children to prosper — to get
their fair share, should they decide to stay

moccasins in two worlds

I am soft, sure footed, flower fragrant
I am the Other, in a confined space
separate, imagined two worlds in one

I am sure of this only, where I stand
is poisoned and I'm conscious of breathing —
breathing in — the garbage we spew

winter is certain

winter is certain

this morning — see, even the geese
are reluctant to follow the rhythm
of nature's long extended hand.
practising formation the loose goose
or two try flying it alone over the river
strongly flowing — *sôhkiciwan*
on this spring-like autumn day.

my breath is visible in this morning's run
recalling a line that words of wisdom
are not the speakers but rather the teaching
of natural laws — resilience in flux

this morning, I know winter is certain
a flat haze of grey surrounding me
a sudden burst of crabapple red, here
pumpkin orange and cranberry berry there
a golden yellow forming as backdrop.

the energy of the sun is distant, cooler
the cold nip of air biting my nose and ears
the signs I read are clear, but even then
I pretend spring — an after midnight stroll
with friends to capture the fragrance of trees
along the banks of the Saskatchewan.

wordsongs of a warrior

what is poetry? how do I explain
this affliction to my mother
in the language she understands,
words strung together, woven
pieces of memory, naming
and telling the truth in a way
that dances, swings and sways

why the subject of my poetry
is sometimes difficult to deliver
why my subjects are terrorized
even controversial, why
the subjects are the essence
of my own being — close to the bone.

nakamowin'sa — wordsongs, I say   wordsongs
kahkiyaw ay'sînôwak kici   for all human beings
ta sohkihtama kipimâsonaw   to give strength on this journey
kitahtawî ayis êkwa   one of these days, for sure now
kam'skâtonanaw   we will find each other

Annie's *caw caw*
(for my mother, Annie)

this morning my mother
is carrying on
the birds too noisy
she couldn't sleep
she says she would like
to take their *caw caw*
and wrap it
around their necks

as I watch her humour us
with her *caw caw* story
she kneads the dough hard
for the fresh bannock
she promises us

I know she's hiding
masking the truth
of her own sadness
a husband buried
a month ago
a sister soon to be

we embrace in laughter
her anger out
on the bannock dough
on the innocent *caw*
caw of the crows

why geese?

la vielle êkwa   the old woman and
son petit vieux   her old man
are back again,
my mother says,
on the drive north.
an expectation
I will understand
the reference
to two old geese
who have returned
to a nearby pond
again this Spring.

when one is gone,
my mother says,
the single one
will return alone
to the same place.
an expectation
I will understand
the reference
to two old friends
who bond forever
in this life
and into the next.

and I wonder
why geese?

heading home

Matilda and Albertine are happy
when I arrive for my daily visit.
they tell me well-rehearsed
the part I will play in the getaway.

Matilda's favourite food is rabbit stew.
Albertine's favourite, *l'frrakasî*   a mixture of meat, onions and potatoes
and bannock slightly browned.
of course, I must ensure
there are enough liquids
to last the journey
water sufficient, perhaps tea.

the next request they make of me
is a hand drawn map
access to highway number eleven
via *nôtin'sîpihk*   the river where a battle took place
heading home to *sâkitawahk*   a place where the land sticks out
their destination, *kîwîtinohk*.   from where the north winds blow

the final detail is yet to be worked out;
slipping through the nurses' station
without being caught. something
Matilida claims with laughter
they can sort out themselves.
this is one secret they refuse to share
even with someone they trust.

I am to meet them with my van
ready to go at the west entrance;
load their wheels and tired bodies;
and set them straight on their way home.
my gift, they say, will be waiting
when I arrive. the place unspoken.

a laugh aloud, Matilda adds
that once on the highway
she will fly a sock half-mast
for the foot that no longer is.
Albertine will fly her breezy bloomers
for a part of the body that won't deliver.

this time they are heading home
home, to stay.

a ritual for goodbye
(in memory of Albertine)

walking the shoreline
this crisp spring morning
in our matching
red line rubber boots
my cousin and I
are reminiscing
the days gone by

I remember first
one early spring
the water so low
we could get
from one island
to the next
our clothes piled high
over our heads

she remembers then
no human debris
like there is now
just the odd
piece of driftwood
she reminded me
we wondered then
where it came from
a guessing game

walking the shoreline
this crisp spring morning
our walk is certain
clinging close
to what we know best
this shoreline, this bond
we don't speak of the fact
that our aunt is dying

earthly matters

when I came to your grave site
late last fall, a chill in the air
I was feeling sorry for myself.
I came looking for a sign
one might say it was —
guidance on earthly matters.

lifting my face skyward
I found nothing but blue sky.
I searched the horizon,
it was then I discovered
a le Bouleau in the distance.
I smiled recalling
that walk we took
through the new cemetery
on a break from city life.
you didn't want to be buried
near the saints anyway
roped in, in a chain link fence.
you were pointing out
as if it were a daily business
family plots here and there.
best of all, you claimed
you had selected the ideal plot
for yourself and your family,
a le Bouleau in the distance.

spring break up

spring break-up will never be the same.
on my vigil late last night I heard
the sound of ice crystals dancing
in the distance. you worrying about me;
my comfort in the chair; my long journey
here from the city alone. I fell asleep
comforted, knowing you would still be
here when I awoke this morning.

the room red from the morning sun,
I listened to you — your breath, fragile.
I waited for you — to catch the first glimpse
of your eyes opening, as if for the last time.
when you did, you wondered aloud, where
that large block of ice, slowly melting
in the middle of the lake had shifted to.

when I told you it was close by — near
the shoreline, in front of your window
you asked to be moved — positioned
so you could see it one last time.

blessed be

she was —
Neruda inspired
wave upon wave
lapping
lapping
against the shoreline.

she read aloud
her own words
for the first time
but only the trees,
the grass and the stones
were there to listen.

standing at the altar
of heaven and earth
she recalled
the unfolding
before her eyes.

blessed be the fisherman
standing at the river's edge
waiting to capture
the slippery glide of a fish.

blessed be the young man
one, with his kayak
skimming the water
to capture the rush of a stormy river.

blessed be a young boy
waving his insect net
chasing the air
to capture the soft stroke of a butterfly.

blessed be the young women
sitting on a rock
mesmerized, reaching out
to capture the vastness of a sky.

blessed be the old woman
sitting in the darkness
gazing deeply
to capture the foreboding night sky.

it was then she saw the hawk
assured, diving to the ground
capturing prey
precisely, swiftly;
a choreograph
of a thousand years.

it was then she noticed
the pelican striking the water
delicately, confidently
capturing the fish;
knowing, rehearsed
timeless movements.

standing there in awe
she bowed.

Some of the poems in this collection were developed as dramatic monologues for the *The Batoche Musical*. Various books, essays and journal articles were re-read, some related to the historical events and issues surrounding the events of the Northwest Resistance of 1885. Authors included Howard Adams, Steven Biko, Harold Cardinal and Walter Hildebrandt, David Dolye, Brian Goehring, bel hooks, the Honourable Alexander Morris, P.C., James McGregor, Guy La vallee, Albert Memmi, Maggie Siggins, Blair Stonechild and Bill Waiser, Linda Smith, Auguste Henri deTremaudan and Rudy Wiebe to name a few.

Excerpts from the monologues were used by actors in *The Batoche Musical* to develop dialogues and songs through improvisational theatre techniques. "letter to a friend" was inspired after re-reading *Father Lacombe* by James G. MacGregor, published by Hurtig Publishers in 1975. "that was a long time ago, and we are here today" was inspired by an essay written by the late Steve Biko titled, "Black Conciousness and the Quest For a True Humanity" (Biko, 1978, *I Write What I Like*, Hienmann Educational Books Ltd). A variation of both "that was a long time ago, and we are here today" and "mama, did god create me?" are performed as part of *The Batoche Musical* each summer at the Back to Batoche Days in Batoche, Saskatchewan. The story for *The Batoche Musical* was created through a writing collective which included Maureen Belanger, Lon Borgersen, Dwayne Favel, Bruce Sinclair, Jack Walton and myself.

Poems which have appeared in literary magazines include "Annie's *caw caw*" and "why geese" in *Prairie Fire*'s, *First Voices, First Words* (2001) edited by Thomas King, the portrait in "The Women of Glenairley" in a chapbook published by Rap Publications (2001) with my Booming Ground poetry pals from across the country with Lorna Crozier as master-teacher, an excerpt from "*kitahtawî êkwa* — one of these days now" was selected by the Saskatchewan Arts

Board and the City of Saskatoon as part of the Poetry in Motion Project, 2002, and "Gabriel Dumont Overture" and "a ritual for goodbye" appeared in *Spring* Volume 111, a publication of the Saskatchewan Writer's Guild.

For this collection, thank you to Lorna Crozier and my Booming Ground poetry pals for the learning and the friendship, thanks to my colleagues with The Batoche Theatre Company, *merci* to Vince Ahenakew of Ile a la Crosse, Saskatchewan, for the michif editing and last but not least *kinanâskomitin* — I thank you, Séan Virgo, for your thoroughness and care in the editing process. *Hâw ninanâskomon!* — now then, I am thankful!

I also want to say thanks to a number people that I neglected to acknowledge in print for their support and valuable advice in the development of my first book of poetry, *Blueberry Clouds* (1999). Thank you, Glen Sorestead, for your advice and generally heading me off in the right direction. Thanks, Maria Campbell, for your gentle prodding and encouragement. Thank you, Al and Paddy (Thistledown Press), for the opportunity you created. Thistledown Press received a nomination to a Saskatchewan Book Award for *Blueberry Clouds*, and "Medicine Man" was selected from this book for an anthology, *Sundog Highway — Writing From Saskatchewan*, edited by Larry Warwaruk and published by Coteau Books. A special thanks to Susan Musgrave for her support and guidance in editing my first book. A special thank you to Paul Jacoby for believing that my voice was worthy of an audience. Thanks to my son, Matt Jacoby! Matthew Joseph, you have inspired me with your sense of humour and playfulness. You are the centre of my universe!